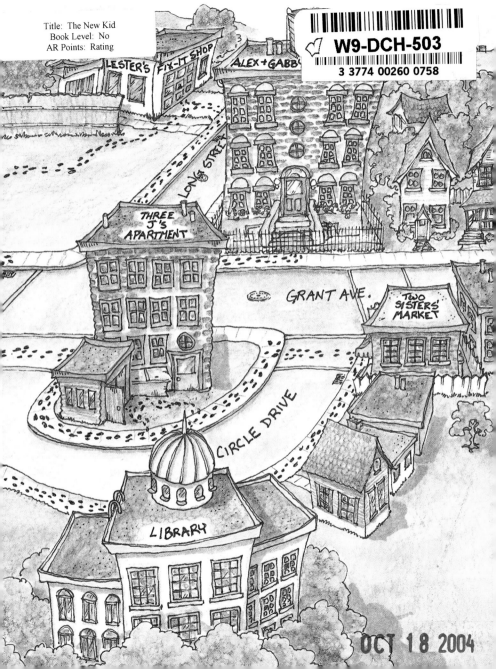

THE NEW KID

Written by Larry Dane Brimner • Illustrated by Christine Tripp

Children's Press®
A Division of Scholastic Inc.
New York • Toronto • London • Auckland • Sydney
Mexico City • New Delhi • Hong Kong
Danbury, Connecticut

For kids everywhere
—L.D.B.

For my friends and neighbors on Fraser Avenue
—C.T.

Library of Congress Cataloging-in-Publication Data

Brimner, Larry Dane.
  The new kid / written by Larry Dane Brimner ; illustrated by Christine
Tripp.
      p. cm.
Summary: Gabby learns a lesson in kindness when she befriends the new
girl in school.
  ISBN 0-516-22546-4 (lib. bdg.)   0-516-27835-5 (pbk.)
  [1. Kindness—Fiction. 2. Friendship—Fiction. 3. Schools—Fiction.]
I. Tripp, Christine, ill. II. Title.
  PZ7.B767 Ne 2003
  [E]—dc21
                              2002008261

This book is about **kindness.**

The Corner Kids hurried into their classroom. Gabby, Alex, and Three J called themselves the Corner Kids because they lived on opposite corners of the same street. They sat down in their chairs.

Mr. Toddle waited for everyone to get quiet. "I want you to meet a new second grade friend," he said. "This is Lisa Lu. I hope everyone will make her feel welcome."

7

The new kid looked down at
her desk.

"She looks afraid," Alex whispered.

Three J nodded, but Gabby did not.
She was drawing a rocket ship.

It was a busy morning. They worked on math and reading and science. Then it was time for lunch.

"There's Lisa," said Alex.

"Let's ask her to sit with us," said Three J.

Gabby didn't like that idea. "It's crowded," she said. "Besides, she's going to sit over there."

As soon as Gabby finished eating, she jumped up. "Hurry, you guys," she said. "Maybe we can get the good ball."

15

The Corner Kids put away their trash. Then they headed for the ball bin.

"Let's ask Lisa to play," said Three J.

17

Gabby grabbed her favorite ball. "But *we* are the Corner Kids," she said. "The three of us."

Three J and Alex both looked sad.

19

"She probably doesn't even live on a corner," Gabby said.

"So? Maybe she'll be fun," said Three J.

Gabby shrugged.

"Remember when you were the new kid at school last year?" asked Three J.

"And remember when you first moved into our apartment building?" asked Alex.

Gabby remembered. She had felt alone and afraid.

Then she met Alex and Three J. They asked her to ride bikes with them around the block. At school, they saved a place for her when it was time for lunch.

25

"You were nice to me," Gabby said quietly. She thought about that. She had been less afraid once she knew Alex and Three J.

27

Gabby looked at Lisa. Lisa *did* look afraid.

"Lisa!" Gabby called. "Do you want to play ball with us?"

29

Lisa smiled. "Sure!" she said.

Gabby smiled, too. Suddenly Lisa didn't look afraid anymore.

31

ABOUT THE AUTHOR

Larry Dane Brimner studied literature and writing at San Diego State University and taught school for twenty years. The author of more than seventy-five books for children, many of them Children's Press titles, he enjoys meeting young readers and writers when he isn't at his computer.

ABOUT THE ILLUSTRATOR

Christine Tripp lives in Ottawa, Canada, with her husband Don; four grown children—Elizabeth, Erin, Emily, and Eric; son-in-law Jason; grandsons Brandon and Kobe; four cats; and one very large, scruffy puppy named Jake.